THE HAUNTED HISTORY OF WASHINGTON, DC

BY CHRISTY MIHALY

An Imprint of Abdo Publishing
abdobooks.com

Cover image: There are three buildings that make up the Library of Congress. Each building is named after a US president.

Printed in the United States of America, North Mankato, Minnesota.
102023
012024

THIS BOOK CONTAINS
RECYCLED MATERIALS

Cover Photo: Leonid Andronov/Shutterstock Images
Interior Photos: powerofforever/DigitalVision Vectors/Getty Images, 4–5; GHI/Universal History Archive/ Universal Images Group/Getty Images, 6; Bettmann/Getty Images, 8; Sarin Images/Granger Historical Picture Archive, 12–13; Everett Collection/Shutterstock Images, 15, 43; Red Line Editorial, 17, 31; Shutterstock Images, 20–21, 25, 40, 45; Artem Avetisyan/Shutterstock Images, 23; Karen Kaspar/Shutterstock Images, 26; Sean Pavone/Shutterstock Images, 28–29; Mark Summerfield/Alamy, 33; Michael S. Williamson/The Washington Post/Getty Images, 36–37

Editors: Priscilla An and Marie Pearson
Series Designer: Ryan Gale

Library of Congress Control Number: 2023939621

Publisher's Cataloging-in-Publication Data
Names: Mihaly, Christy, author.
Title: The haunted history of Washington, DC / by Christy Mihaly
Description: Minneapolis, Minnesota: Abdo Publishing, 2024 | Series: Haunted history of the United States | Includes online resources and index.
Identifiers: ISBN 9781098292553 (lib. bdg.) | ISBN 9798384910497 (ebook)
Subjects: LCSH: Haunted places--United States--Juvenile literature. | History--Juvenile literature. | Ghosts-- United States--Juvenile literature. | Washington (D.C.)--History--Juvenile literature.
Classification: DDC 133.109--dc23

CONTENTS

ABRAHAM LINCOLN'S GHOST

One day in the 1920s, First Lady Grace Coolidge reported seeing President Abraham Lincoln's ghost. She was in the family quarters on the second floor of the White House, walking by the Yellow Oval Room. Tall windows in the room provide a view of the South Lawn. Decades before, President Lincoln had used the Yellow Oval Room as his library.

On this day, it seemed Lincoln was still there. Coolidge glimpsed his tall, dark figure standing by the windows. He wore all

Abraham Lincoln was president from 1861 until his death in 1865.

black and a shawl over his shoulders as if to keep warm.

Hands clasped behind his back, he stared out the

window across the Potomac River toward Virginia.

Lincoln's ghost turned to look at her for a moment, then

vanished. Coolidge is often said to be the first White

House resident to report seeing Lincoln's ghost.

THE LINCOLN BEDROOM AND BEYOND

The White House in Washington, DC, is the home of US presidents and their families. It also has a reputation for being the home of numerous ghosts. Coolidge's story is one of many reported appearances of President Lincoln's ghost. As president, Lincoln led the country through the American Civil War (1861–1865). The Southern states, worried that the Northern states wanted to outlaw slavery, withdrew from the United States, forming the Confederacy. Lincoln led the fight to reunite the country and eventually to end slavery.

Abraham Lincoln's office was in what is now the Lincoln Bedroom in the White House.

He grieved the thousands of lives lost during the war. Lincoln often stood at his library window looking out toward the Virginia battlefields in the same posture that Coolidge described.

The space Lincoln used for his office and meetings is now used as a bedroom. People call it the Lincoln Bedroom. Many consider the room to be haunted. Over the years, numerous people, and perhaps some animals, have sensed Lincoln's ghost there.

First Lady Eleanor Roosevelt occupied the White House with her husband Franklin Roosevelt in the 1930s and 1940s. She said she often felt Lincoln's presence there. One day her secretary fled the room after she believed she saw Lincoln sitting on the bed pulling on his boots.

President Ronald Reagan lived in the White House in the 1980s. Reagan's adult daughter Maureen and her husband, Dennis, regularly slept in the Lincoln Bedroom. Dennis told Maureen

PERSPECTIVES

BELIEVING IN GHOSTS

Pamela Apkarian-Russell visited the White House in 1969 with her aunt, who worked there. Walking down a hall, they both thought they saw a tall figure wearing black. Then he disappeared. They recognized it as Abraham Lincoln's ghost.

Apkarian-Russell's experience inspired her to study and research the ghosts of Washington, DC. She wrote a book called *Washington's Haunted Past*. In her book, she notes that many people refuse to believe in ghosts. She points out that denying that something exists does not make it disappear.

he'd seen a ghostly figure there one night. Maureen did not believe him until later when she woke up to see a figure staring out the window. Then she realized she could see through the figure. President Reagan also said the family dog, Rex, barked at the Lincoln Bedroom door and then refused to enter the room. Reagan wondered whether Rex could see Lincoln's ghost.

The White House and the nation's capital city of Washington, DC, have seen more than 200 years of wars, violent deaths, historic events, and passionate disputes between people in the government. Such events are said to have the potential to result in hauntings. One theory is that ghosts return to places where strong emotions were experienced during life. Another theory says that some ghosts appear because they left behind unfinished business or because they want to correct an injustice. Some say that people invent ghost stories. Whatever the explanation, the rich history of Washington, DC, has given rise to an abundance of ghost stories.

STRAIGHT TO THE
SOURCE

In 1946, President Harry Truman wrote to his wife, Bess, while she was away, describing nighttime events at the White House:

Night before last I went to bed at nine o'clock after shutting all my doors. At four o'clock I was awakened by three distinct knocks on my bedroom door. I jumped up and put on my bathrobe, opened the door, and no one there. Went out and looked up and down the hall, looked into your room. . . . Still no one. Went back to bed after locking the doors and there were footsteps in your room whose door I'd left open. Jumped and looked and no one there! The . . . place is haunted sure as shootin'. Secret service said not even a watchman was up here at that hour.

Source: "Letter from Harry S. Truman to Bess W. Truman, September 9, 1946." *Harry S. Truman Library and Museum*, n.d., trumanlibrary.gov. Accessed 30 Mar. 2023.

CHANGING MINDS

Take a position on whether the White House is haunted and imagine that your best friend has the opposite opinion. Write a short essay trying to change your friend's mind. Make sure to explain your opinion and your reasons for it. Include facts and details that support your reasons.

HAUNTED WHITE HOUSE

John Adams was the first president to live in the White House. He moved into the building in 1800 with his wife, Abigail. The mansion has undergone many changes since then. In 1814, British soldiers set it afire when they invaded Washington during the War of 1812. The stone walls withstood the fire, but the interior was destroyed. The White House was rebuilt, and since then it has been remodeled and expanded several more times. Since Adams, all the US presidents, their families, and many workers have lived there.

The White House has been through many changes over time.

Numerous White House residents have felt the presence of those who came before them. First Lady Mary Todd Lincoln reported hearing former president Andrew Jackson swearing and stomping around in the building. In life, Jackson was known for his bad temper. White House residents also reported hearing shouting and laughing that they attributed to Jackson's ghost.

Lincoln's assassination left Mary Todd Lincoln overcome with sorrow. She sought comfort in spiritualism, as she had after Willie's death. In about 1870, Mary visited William H. Mumler, a "spirit photographer," who claimed to capture spirits on film. The photograph he took shows Mary seated in a chair. The ghostly image of Lincoln appears behind her, his hands resting on her shoulders. Nobody at the time could figure out exactly how Mumler created his spirit photographs. In any event, this picture provided great comfort to Mary.

MARY'S SEARCH FOR SPIRITS

Mary Todd Lincoln also believed she saw

Willie, *right*, died of typhoid fever, a disease caused by bacteria.

the ghost of her son, Willie. In 1862, 11-year-old Willie became sick and died in the White House. In her grief, Mary turned to spiritualism, which is based on the belief that the living can communicate with the dead. Spiritualism became widespread during the Civil War, as many grieving families went to mediums hoping to contact the spirits of their loved ones.

Mary started hosting spirit circles, or séances, in the White House, asking mediums to reach out to

Willie's spirit. Mary later told her sister that they had succeeded and that the ghost of Willie had appeared to her. Many nights, she said, Willie stood by her bed and smiled. He sometimes brought along his brother Eddie, who had died years earlier. According to the White House Historical Association, when Ulysses S. Grant was president in the 1870s, others in the White House also believed they saw Willie's ghost.

MYSTERIES AND LEGENDS

Unexplained events have continued to occur in the current century. George W. Bush and his family occupied the White House from 2001 to 2009. Twin daughters Barbara and Jenna Bush had a haunting experience that Jenna later shared in television interviews. They woke up in the middle of the night and heard mysterious music coming from the bedroom fireplace. Jenna described it as piano music from the 1920s. A week or so later, the same thing happened with opera music. The sisters never located a radio or

HAUNTED
HOUSE

Some of the reported hauntings are shown on this White House floor plan. The White House has been remodeled over time, so locations may be approximate. How does the floor plan help your understanding of possible White House hauntings?

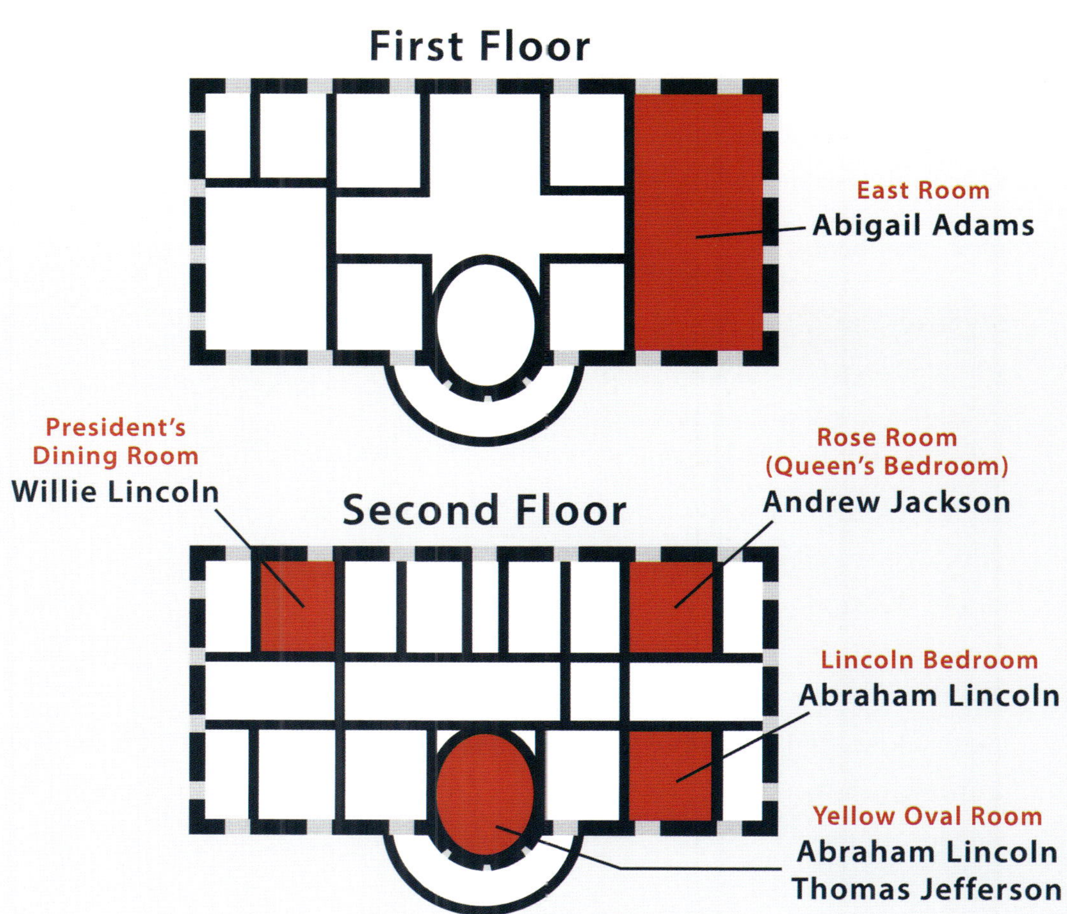

PERSPECTIVES

ARE THE GHOSTS FRIENDLY?

Former White House head usher Gary Walters believes the White House ghosts are friendly. Walters worked for several presidents over the years and has overseen White House operations. On Halloween 2013, he answered haunting questions from the public on the White House website.

Someone asked him whether the White House ghosts were friendly. Walters said, "Absolutely." He said all the presidents he had worked for felt positive about whatever spirits were present in the White House. Living in this historic home, in the same spaces as prior presidents, made them feel a close bond with those who came before them.

identified the source of the music. Although it was creepy, they decided to assume the musical ghost was friendly.

There are many other legendary White House phantoms. Among them are the ghosts of First Lady Abigail Adams hanging her laundry in the East Room and First Lady Dolley Madison guarding her rose garden from meddling gardeners. There is said to be a lost British soldier from the War of 1812 wandering the White House grounds. Some have said they heard Thomas Jefferson playing his violin. And a White House worker once reported that President William Henry Harrison's ghost haunted the attic.

Over the years, the White House has witnessed a great deal of history. Some people believe this history may be why there are so many reports of ghosts and unexplained activity there. This is also why people believe other places in Washington, DC, are haunted.

GHOSTS UNDER THE DOME

The dome of the US Capitol Building rises above Capitol Hill. It stands as a proud symbol of the spirit of democracy. The events that have unfolded under the dome have reflected the nation's history and have also inspired stories of ghostly spirits.

The tale of John Quincy Adams stands out among the Capitol ghost stories. Adams was the sixth president of the United States. After leaving the presidency, Adams served in the House of Representatives for 17 years. He was called Old Man Eloquent and was

The US Capitol was once intended to be the burial place for George Washington.

known for giving fiery speeches. Adams opposed going to war against Mexico in the Mexican-American War (1846–1848) and was also a leading opponent of slavery. In 1848 at the age of 80, Adams collapsed during a House debate. He was taken to a nearby room in the Capitol, where he received care until he died two days later.

It is rumored that Adams's spirit remains in the Old House Chamber, the site of his

The Old House Chamber is now the Statuary Hall.

last debate. Steve Livengood, historian and chief guide of the United States Capitol Historical Society, reported seeing Adams's ghost there. Other witnesses say they have heard Old Man Eloquent shouting "No!" as he continues making his speech to Congress.

WORKERS WHO REMAIN

The ghosts of lesser-known people have also been reported in the Capitol. One of these is Bishop

PERSPECTIVES

CONGRESSPEOPLE SPEAK

In 2009, a reporter for the *Hill* asked members of Congress if they had seen ghosts in the Capitol. Most denied believing in ghosts. But New York congressman José Serrano responded that he sometimes felt ghostly company surrounding him. He said, "When I sit in the [House] chair at times, I know that there are members around" besides those physically present for the vote. Nancy Pelosi, longtime Speaker of the House, said the Capitol sometimes "feels haunted," though she had not seen a ghost. And Vermont senator Patrick Leahy said a ghost would sometimes move a 300-pound (136-kg) table when nobody was around.

John Sims. He ran the Senate barbershop for decades, through the 1930s. Born into slavery, Sims escaped during the Civil War and later became both a barber and the pastor of a local church. He was a beloved figure who gave senators haircuts regardless of their party membership. He often gave them good advice as well. He sang gospel tunes while working. Sims died in 1934. Livengood is among those who

Unexplained music and singing are among the more common paranormal experiences.

have heard Sims's ghost singing in the hallway near his former barbershop.

Thousands of people have labored to build, clean, repair, and care for the Capitol building over the years.

Some say there are workers who chose to stay on after death. Witnesses describe hearing a ghostly Capitol cleaner still scrubbing the marble floors after hours. Others believe they have spotted the phantoms of craftspeople who died in accidents during Capitol construction from the 1790s through the 1860s. A common theme among many Capitol hauntings is that those who served there were dedicated to their work and were perhaps unable to leave a task unfinished.

STRAIGHT TO THE
SOURCE

On September 28, 1984, the *New York Times* published an article about Senator Patrick Leahy occupying his new Capitol hideaway, an unmarked room that serves as a senator's private retreat:

> *Senator Patrick J. Leahy, for one, is taking no chances. The Vermont Democrat says he is not afraid of ghosts, not even that of Daniel Webster, who, so legend has it, still roams the vaulted room that Senator Leahy recently [claimed as his] hideaway.*
>
> *But, just in case, Mr. Leahy has named the room the Daniel Webster Memorial Room and has duly addressed to Senator Daniel Webster an invitation to a dedication. . . .*
>
> *After all, it was that mighty 19th-century orator and statesman who, on his deathbed in 1852, solemnly proclaimed: "I still live."*
>
> Source: Marjorie Hunter. "Appeasing Daniel Webster's Ghost." *New York Times*, 28 Sept. 1984, nytimes.com. Accessed 5 Apr. 2023.

WHAT'S THE BIG IDEA?

Read the text carefully. What is the main idea? How is the main idea supported by details? Name two or three supporting details.

CREEPY DC

The White House and the Capitol aren't the only haunted spots in DC. Spirits have been sighted in old homes from grand mansions to tiny cottages. Other sites reported to be haunted are a theater, an army post, a library, and more.

GHOSTS OF LINCOLN'S ASSASSINATION

Many stories swirl about the assassination of Abraham Lincoln. John Wilkes Booth shot the president during a play in Ford's Theatre on April 14, 1865. More than 150 years later, when

Lincoln was assassinated in the box seats, *upper left,* **in Ford's Theatre.**

plays are presented at Ford's Theatre, spooky things happen. Some actors have sensed a presence onstage. Others have seen a ghostly figure in the seat where Lincoln sat. Some have heard running feet backstage, which are said to be the footsteps of the assassin.

Eight people were convicted in the conspiracy to kill Lincoln. One was Mary Surratt. She ran the boardinghouse where Booth and the others met to coordinate their plans, and one of the accused men testified

HOPELESS?

The stunning deep-blue Hope Diamond is a popular exhibit at the National Museum of Natural History in DC. This beautiful walnut-sized gem was donated to the museum in 1958. Some people believe it carries a curse. The diamond's last private owner was DC resident Evalyn Walsh McLean. She acquired it in 1911. Eight years later, her nine-year-old son was killed by a car. Many previous owners also met unfortunate fates. Among them, Queen Marie Antoinette and King Louis XVI of France were beheaded. Other owners suffered financial ruin, mental illness, and painful diseases. Some people say these events were just coincidence, but others blame the diamond.

HAUNTED
DC MAP

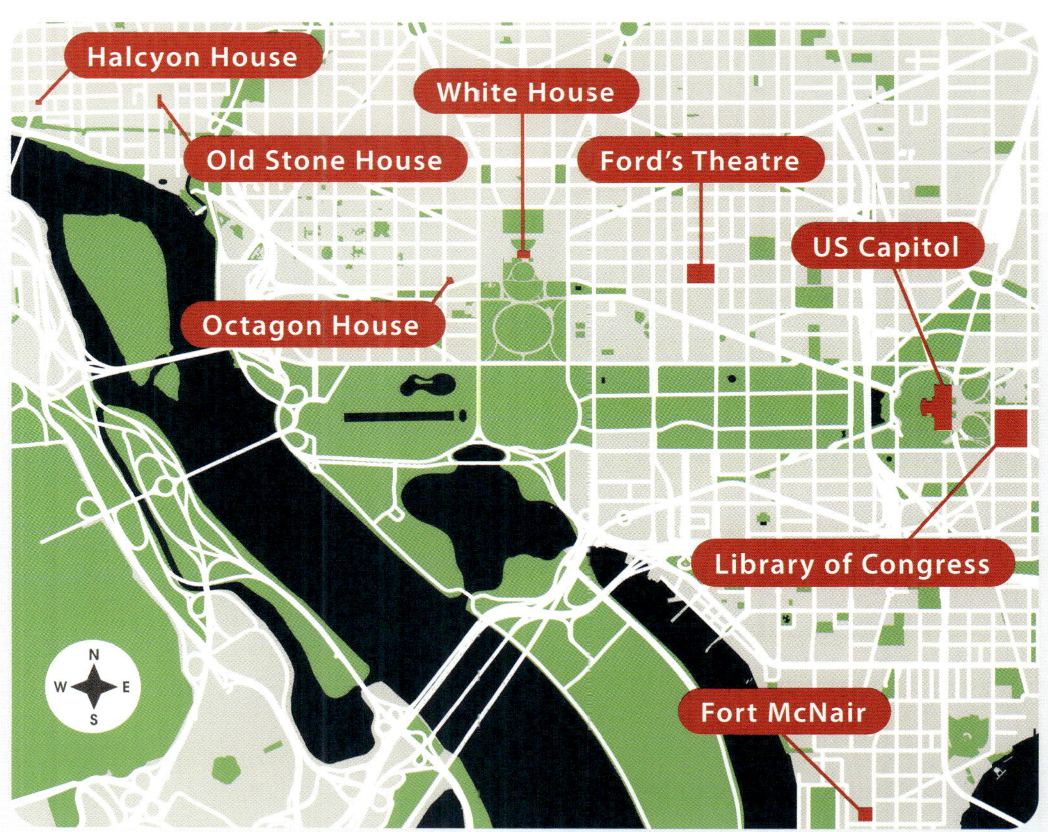

that she helped in the plot. However, some people have questioned whether Surratt was guilty. Nonetheless, she was sentenced to death by hanging. She protested her sentence, perhaps even after death. Surratt and three others were hung at DC's Fort McNair. A 1991 *Washington Post* article described the appearance of a black-clad phantom at the historic fort, which many believe is Surratt's ghost. An honor guard at Fort McNair said that more than once he saw a clear path mysteriously melted through the deep snow. The path was 2 feet (0.6 m) wide and followed the route that Surratt took on her final walk from the jail to the gallows, a structure used for hanging people.

GHOSTS AROUND TOWN

Not all DC ghosts have dark backstories. Some say ghostly parties are happening in the capital. In 1814, while the White House was undergoing repairs, President James Madison and his wife, Dolley, moved into a nearby mansion, the Octagon House.

Though an actual octagon has eight sides, the Octagon House has six sides. They are positioned to match the tight angle of the street corner.

Dolley hosted wonderful parties there. Years later, after her death, newspapers reported she was still throwing parties. People said they saw footmen in old-fashioned dress flagging down carriages for guests and heard carriages bumping along the street outside the Octagon House. Some said they saw Dolley's ghost inside by

PERSPECTIVES

HALCYON HOUSE

Halcyon House is a regular stop on DC's "ghost tours." Albert Clemens, who lived there in the 1930s, had many odd beliefs. He hated electricity and banned it from his house. Canden Arciniega works for a DC tour company. One night in about 2014, she led a walking tour outside the empty Halcyon House. As she explained that a ghost in a wide-brimmed hat sometimes appeared at a window, the streetlamp suddenly went out. Then the group saw a shadowy figure wearing a wide-brimmed hat in the window. They ran away, screaming. "I've seen it with my own eyes, and it still stalks me," Arciniega said. After this incident, streetlights kept dimming when Arciniega passed.

the fireplace. And the scent of lilacs, Dolley's favorite, is said to linger in the house.

Other hauntings have been reported at the Library of Congress. The country's national library contains history, millions of books, and perhaps a few ghosts. Some people say the library hosts the spirits of a helpful police officer and one or more former library workers still hard at work.

The Old Stone House is one of the

oldest buildings in Washington, DC. It was built around 1766. This tiny house is rumored to be crowded with ten or more ghosts. They include a ghostly woman standing by the fireplace, another in a rocking chair, and a boy running down a hallway. Then there's George, a mean spirit. This ghost has been blamed for choking and pushing visitors. The Old Stone House is open to the public, though not for ghost tours.

EXPLORE ONLINE

Chapter Four talks about the assassination of Abraham Lincoln. The article at the website below goes into more depth on this topic. Does the article answer any of the questions you had about Lincoln's assassination?

LINCOLN'S ASSASSINATION

abdocorelibrary.com/haunted-washington-dc

WHAT'S GOING ON?

Paranormal investigators suggest that the intense emotions from dramatic past events can cause a place to be haunted. They say that strong feelings cause a ghostly energy to be imprinted on the location. This may be a possible explanation for some of the hauntings in Washington, DC. In other cases, ghost stories are just stories.

Some ghost stories are legends, which are stories that contain elements of truth but have changed over time into fictional tales. Some may have changed to include the paranormal.

The Congressional Cemetery in DC is one of many other haunted locations in the capital city.

FACT-CHECKING A GREAT STORY

During World War II (1939–1945), British prime minister Winston Churchill had meetings with President Franklin Roosevelt to coordinate their efforts against the Nazis. Churchill slept at the White House. A ghost story has been retold about his overnight visit. Churchill took a late-night bath. Naked, he walked into the adjoining bedroom. There he encountered Lincoln's ghost, fully clothed. Churchill greeted Lincoln politely, saying the president seemed to have him at a disadvantage. However, historian Richard Langworth says this story is untrue. He points out that Churchill didn't stay in the Lincoln Bedroom, didn't take baths late at night, and never told this story himself.

For example, in 1963, when President Lyndon B. Johnson and his family moved into the White House, his daughter Lynda got the room that Willie Lincoln had used. Later, many sources claimed that Lynda saw Willie's ghost there and even talked with him. Finally, an investigator asked her about this. Lynda clarified that she had researched and discussed the history of her room, but she never saw Willie's ghost.

SPOOKY SOUNDS AND STORIES

Sometimes there are natural explanations for seemingly supernatural events. For example, many ghost stories feature scary noises. In the US Capitol, sounds echo along empty hallways and bounce from high ceilings. Security guards report hearing footsteps and other strange sounds. But not all spooky sounds are ghosts.

One popular Capitol story is that a demon cat stalks the halls with haunting howls. There are even mysterious cat footprints imprinted on the Capitol floor. Capitol guards working at night started spreading stories about the spooky cat in the late 1800s. They said they were attacked by a black cat that grew to a gigantic size, then disappeared. Some people warned that when this cat appeared, it meant a national catastrophe would occur.

Livengood dug into this tale and concluded that there was no demon cat. Instead, he said the story originated with regular cats and security guards. Until the early 1900s, cats were kept in the Capitol basement. They were brought in to keep the building's

People have historically associated black cats with bad luck or Satanic rituals.

rat population under control. Livengood believes a night watchman was lying down on the job when one of the resident cats came up and licked his face. The guard woke up suddenly, believing he was still standing, and concluded he had been attacked by a monster cat. As for the cat footprints, it seems that one cat walked across wet cement when a section of the flooring was replaced.

Nighttime noises have haunted the White House too. Old houses often creak as they settle. When President Truman moved in, he noticed the building made so many strange noises that he became concerned it was falling apart. Engineers discovered the structure was in such bad shape it was in danger of collapse.

Renovations began in 1948 and finished four years later. The repairs probably reduced the nighttime noises in the White House. But they did not stop the ghost sightings. Indeed, in the White House, the Capitol, and elsewhere in Washington, DC, people continue to feel the presence of the past.

GHOST STORIES

Historical researcher Colleen Shogan has a theory about why people tell White House ghost stories. She says many ghost stories involve unfinished business or an injustice. Because President Lincoln died at the beginning of his second term, much was unresolved. Lincoln was unable to complete his task of bringing the nation together after the Civil War. Shogan says people like to think of Lincoln remaining in the White House. The stories of his ghostly presence help Americans come to terms with a troubled history.

FAST FACTS

- Presidents, first ladies, and White House staff have reported seeing ghosts or feeling a ghostly presence in the White House. The most famous such ghost is Abraham Lincoln's.

- White House ghost sightings besides Lincoln include Andrew Jackson, Abigail Adams, Dolley Madison, Thomas Jefferson, William Henry Harrison, a British soldier, and Willie Lincoln.

- In the US Capitol, the ghost of John Quincy Adams has been seen haunting the spot where he collapsed on the floor of the Old House Chamber.

- People say that ghostly singing in the Capitol is the spirit of Bishop John Sims, a barber and pastor who worked in the Senate barbershop.

- Ghost stories are told about many Washington, DC, houses, including the Halcyon House, Octagon House, and Old Stone House.

- The ghost of Mary Surratt is said to haunt Fort McNair, where she was executed for conspiring to assassinate President Lincoln. Stories say that Ford's Theatre, where the president was shot, hosts the ghost of assassin John Wilkes Booth.

- There may be natural explanations for some supposedly supernatural events. Some White House noises were the result of the building falling into disrepair. The story about the demon cat in the Capitol probably arose from real cats and incorrect stories told by guards.

- Some ghostly legends start with an element of truth but grow into fictional tales.

STOP AND THINK

Why Do I Care?

Chapter Two includes a section on young Willie Lincoln and his ghost. It describes the efforts his mother took to try to see him again. Have you or someone you know ever lost a loved one? Why might people find comfort in the thought of the person's spirit visiting them?

You Are There

This book discusses different reports of ghosts in the White House. Imagine you are living in the White House and that you experienced something that could be supernatural. Write a letter to a friend about your eerie White House encounter. Be sure to add plenty of detail to your notes.

Dig Deeper

After reading this book, what questions do you still have about Lincoln's assassination? With an adult's help, find a few reliable sources that can help you answer your questions. Write a paragraph about what you learned.

Say What?

Learning about hauntings and history can mean learning
a lot of new vocabulary. Find five words in this book that
you've never heard before. Use a dictionary to find out what
they mean. Then write the definitions in your own words and
use each word in a new sentence.

GLOSSARY

assassination
the murder of a person who is important or famous, such as a president

eloquent
speaking or writing well, in a way that convinces people of an argument or point

medium
a person who claims to communicate with the spirits of dead people

paranormal
events that can't be explained by science

phantom
a ghost or an imagined figure

séance
a gathering at which people try to contact the spirits of the dead, often with a medium

spiritualism
a belief system involving communication with the spirits of the dead, especially with the help of mediums

supernatural
outside of normal human experience or knowledge, or outside the laws of nature

vaulted
built with arches, as in a roof or ceiling

ONLINE RESOURCES

To learn more about hauntings and Washington, DC, visit our free resource websites below.

Visit **abdocorelibrary.com** or scan this QR code for free Common Core resources for teachers and students, including vetted activities, multimedia, and booklinks, for deeper subject comprehension.

Visit **abdobooklinks.com** or scan this QR code for free additional online weblinks for further learning. These links are routinely monitored and updated to provide the most current information available.

LEARN MORE

Rumsch, BreAnn. *Abraham Lincoln*. Abdo, 2021.

Sebra, Richard. *Washington, DC*. Abdo, 2023.

Spalding, Maddie. *Ghosts*. ReferencePoint Press, 2022.

INDEX

About the Author

Christy Mihaly is an award-winning author who has written more than 30 nonfiction books for young readers. A former lawyer, she particularly enjoys writing about the United States government, as well as history and science. She has visited many of the Washington, DC, sites discussed in this book, although she has not yet seen a ghost. Mihaly lives with her family in Vermont.